WILTSHIRE
TRACTION

Mark Jamieson

AMBERLEY

First published 2018

Amberley Publishing
The Hill, Stroud
Gloucestershire, GL5 4EP

www.amberley-books.com

Copyright © Mark Jamieson, 2018

The right of Mark Jamieson to be identified as
the Author of this work has been asserted in
accordance with the Copyrights, Designs and
Patents Act 1988.

ISBN 978 1 4456 7177 2 (print)
ISBN 978 1 4456 7178 9 (ebook)

British Library Cataloguing in Publication Data.
A catalogue record for this book is available from
the British Library.

Origination by Amberley Publishing.
Printed in the UK.

Introduction

In the 1861 edition of *Bradshaw's Handbook of Great Britain and Ireland*, as featured in the television series *Great British Railway Journeys* presented by Michael Portillo, George Bradshaw describes Wiltshire as:

> An inland and fertile county, divided into South and North. The aspect of the former displays considerable beauty, as the principal valleys in this division of Wiltshire lie along the banks of the rivers, the most remarkable of which diverge, like irregular radii, from the country around Salisbury and Wilton, these display rich meadows and corn land, interspersed with towns, private residences and extensive plantation of wood.
>
> North Wiltshire differs completely from the southern division of the county. Instead of the gentle undulations of the south, it appears a complete level and is so thickly wooded that at a short distance it resembles a one vast plantation of trees. When examined in detail, however, it is found to contain many fertile and richly cultivated spots. The chief commodities are sheep, wool, wood and stone, and the principal manufacturers are in the different branches of the clothing trade.

Bounded by the counties of Hampshire, Somerset, Berkshire, Dorset, Oxfordshire and Gloucestershire, the county of Wiltshire has several significant main line railway routes passing through it.

To the north of the county the Great Western Main Line runs from London Paddington to South Wales, through the heart of the county with the Berks & Hants route from Reading to Westbury, and westwards towards Taunton. To the south of the county the former London & South Western Railway route runs from London Waterloo to Exeter.

The cross-country route from Southampton to Bath cuts across the county from the south-east to the north-west. Wiltshire is also home to the Great Western Railway town of Swindon, although sadly a shadow of its former past. The Brunel-built workshops at Swindon – closed by British Rail on 26 March 1986 – along with the site and its listed-status buildings have been developed as a retail outlet with new housing built within the site. English Heritage have their headquarters in the former engineers' office and a railway presence remains on-site in the form of the Swindon Steam Railway Museum. Swindon is also the junction with the route via Kemble and Stroud to Standish Junction, often referred to as 'the golden valley'.

The cathedral city of Salisbury, in the south of the county, still provides an important interchange between services on the Cardiff to Portsmouth route as well as those between London Waterloo and Exeter St Davids. A depot was provided for the new Class 159 units that would work the Waterloo to Exeter service from mid-1993 on the site of the former

GWR station at Salisbury. Salisbury enjoys its best ever service to London with a half-hourly service covering the 83-mile journey in ninety minutes. The county town of Trowbridge is served by services on the Portsmouth to Cardiff route, as well as the Westbury to Swindon route via Melksham, with Class 166 units.

The county of Wiltshire is principally served by two major passenger train operating companies: Great Western Railway (GWR) – owned by First Group – and South Western Railway (SWR) – a collaboration between First Group (70 per cent) and the Hong Kong MTR Corporation (30 per cent).

The GWR is gradually phasing in their new Hitachi-built Class 800 units to replace the HST sets, which have served the route well since the 1970s.

Class 166 Thames Turbo units from the Reading area are gradually replacing Class 150 and 158 units on the Bristol to Westbury, Southampton and Weymouth routes as part of an ongoing programme of displacement and upgrade in connection with the much publicised Great Western main line electrification from Paddington to Bristol and South Wales.

The South Western Railway continues to use the Class 158 and 159 units that have served the Waterloo to Salisbury and Exeter route since 1993, as well as the service from Salisbury to Bristol.

The major freight operator in Wiltshire is the German-owned DB Cargo (DBC), formerly English Welsh & Scottish (EWS). Operating from a major rail freight centre at Westbury, DBC is the most significant operator here. Synonymous with the Westbury area, the small fleet of Class 59s operate the numerous stone workings out of the Mendip quarries to such destinations as Acton Yard, Woking, Fareham, Chichester, Eastleigh, Poole, Royal Wootton Bassett, Avonmouth and Exeter.

In recent years, other operators have started to penetrate deep into this DBC stronghold; in particular Colas Railfreight, which now operates regularly from Westbury, principally on engineering trains.

GB Railfreight (GBRf) has also started to operate a regular flow from the yard and, for the first time, an operator other than DBC has started working into Whatley Quarry with an irregular train from Wellingborough, which generally runs one week in four, this also being GBRf operated.

In eastern Wiltshire lies Ludgershall, on the former Midland & South Western Junction Railway from Andoversford to Andover via Cirencester, Swindon and Marlborough. After gradual closure of the line, only the section from Ludgershall to Andover would remain for use by military freight traffic.

In northern Wiltshire, Swindon sees regular through freight traffic, principally by DBC, Freightliner and Colas Railfreight. A twice-daily engineers' trip between the yards of Westbury and Eastleigh, worked by DBC and Colas Railfreight, brings much welcomed freight traffic through the Wylye Valley, which also sees stone traffic to and from the former Southern Region, as well as occasional Freightliner traffic.

Covering the last thirty-five years or so, this book hopes to include some of the diverse workings, and traction, that have passed through the county – from the days of British Rail to the privatised railway of today.

Thanks to Connor Stait and the team at Amberley Publishing for their understanding over the last twelve months or so. As always, I could not have done this without the contributions of others so a big thank you to Steve McMullin, Nic Joynson, Tom Curtis, Tony Callaghan, Andrew P. M. Wright, Steve King, Dan Read, Mark Pike, Steve Clark and John Dedman.

Mark Jamieson

Still looking good at forty years old, sadly the days of the High Speed Train (HST) on Great Western are soon to change forever with the eventual introduction of the heavily delayed electrification between London and Bristol or South Wales, bringing with it new trains. On 3 October 2016, 1C81, the 11.33 Paddington–Exeter St Davids, led by power car No. 43069, approaches Fairwood Junction. Power car No. 43180 trails to the rear. (Author)

South West Trains Class 159 No. 159021 passes Wylye while working 1V33, the 13.52 Salisbury–Bristol Temple Meads service on 4 May 2016. There are about five weekday services on the Salisbury to Westbury line operated by South Western Railway to Bristol or Yeovil. (Author)

Traversing the 8-mile single line section between Thingley Junction and Bradford Junction is No. 59202 *Alan Meadows Taylor – MD Mendip Rail Limited*, which is seen approaching Melksham on 24 February 2015 with 6C48, the 13.30 Appleford–Whatley Quarry service. This small fleet of six Class 59/2 locomotives are outbased from Toton depot to Westbury, specifically for working stone trains to and from the Mendip quarries alongside the local Class 59s. (Author)

Running about 73 minutes early, No. 59002 *Alan J. Day* approaches Fairwood Junction on 27 February 2015 while working 7C31, the 09.12 Theale–Merehead stone empties. Note the EWS-liveried ex-coal hoppers, a result in the downturn of coal trains since the closure of several power stations, including the likes of Didcot 'A', now used for aggregate traffic. (Author)

Former Stratford favourite No. 47581 *Great Eastern* stands at Salisbury on 2 June 1990 with Saturdays-only 1V10, 09.07 Brighton–Plymouth. Although a Network SouthEast sector locomotive, therefore placing it in the right part of the world and on a suitable service, it rarely strayed onto the Southern Region, making this a rare outing for this particular Class 47. (Author)

Crossing the River Avon at Bradford-on-Avon on 30 May 1989 is this DMU working a Weymouth to Bristol service. (Nic Joynson)

Passing the site of the former Wolfhall Junction on 31 July 1986 is No. 50032 *Courageous* with 1C39, the 11.45 Paddington–Penzance train. Above the locomotive can be seen the embankment of the former Midland & South Western Junction Railway (M&SWJR) line (later absorbed by the GWR from 29 October 1923) that ran from Andoversford Junction, near Cheltenham, to Red Post Junction, near Andover, via Cirencester, Swindon Town, Marlborough and Ludgershall, crossing over the GWR Berks & Hants route here at Wolfhall. The line was to close in sections, with this section from Marlborough to Grafton South Junction closing during 1959 (last train was 13 September 1958). Wolfhall Junction and its connecting line to Grafton South Junction was taken out of use during 1961 and the signal box, which would have been to the right of the Class 50, would finally close on 22 November 1964. (Tony Callaghan)

About 5 miles to the east of Salisbury lies the village of East Grimstead, close to the Hampshire border. On 27 March 2017, Freightliner's No. 66540 *Ruby* passes with 4M68, the 14.14 Southampton Maritime–Garston Freightliner Terminal. This is one of several Freightliner trains routed out of Southampton via Romsey, Laverstock and Andover then back on to the more familiar route at Worting Junction near Basingstoke. (Author)

Trials to move flyash originating from Langannet power station by rail commenced during May 1997 to Westbury; prior to this, deliveries were by road. Initially, wagons were conveyed via the Parc Slip to Westbury Cement Works coal trains but by July 1997 the flyash operated as a separate working. Loaded/empty wagons worked to and from Longannet via the Mossend enterprise trip to Newport ADJ and onwards to Westbury. On 10 November 1998, Loadhaul-liveried No. 37516 is pictured at Bradford-on-Avon with the return working; 6B73, the 12.20 Westbury Cement Works–Newport ADJ with the empty PCA type wagons. (Steve McMullin)

First Great Western's No. 150131 passes Upton Scudamore on 21 April 2015 while working 2E27, the 17.28 Warminster–Great Malvern service. (Author)

Stunning autumnal weather on 2 November 2016 in the Wylye Valley. Passing the idyllic location of Little Langford is No. 150234, with its recently applied Great Western Railway green livery, working 2O05, the 11.11 Westbury–Southampton Central 'stopper'. (Author)

On 31 May 1991, Derby research Class 47 No. 47974 was named *The Permanent Way Institute* at Newcastle station. Six days later, on 6 June 1991, the Class 47 is seen at Bradford Junction with vintage observation saloon GE1 running as 2Z01 (the 09.11 Swindon–Swansea via Taunton and Bristol observation special). To the right the former Bradford Junction signal box can just be seen; this was closed on 17 March 1990. Having been stood redundant for a day shy of two years, the GWR Type 11 structure was demolished on 16 March 1992, then buried in a pit. (Steve McMullin)

After a loco change at Westbury on Winfrith-bound flasks, which would normally see either a Class 33, 37, 47 or 73 take the movement onwards, it was No. 73134 *Woking Homes 1885–1985* and No. 73126 *Kent & East Sussex Railway* that would be diagrammed for this duty on 10 September 1992. Here, the pair pass Old Dilton with 7Z00, the 09.47 Bridgwater–Winfrith flask, while the tail end of an Eastleigh to Merehead stone train can be seen in the distance. (Steve McMullin)

Power car No. 43169 *The National Trust* on the approach to Westbury on 30 October 2017 at Fairwood while working 1A82, the 11.32 Paignton–Paddington. Power car No. 43012 *Exeter Panel Signal Box 21st Anniversary* trails along behind. (Author)

No. 66131 passes Crofton on 11 October 2011 working 6M20, the 11.37 Whatley Quarry–St Pancras train, formed of orange RMC hoppers. (Author)

Power car No. 43197 leads 1A77, the 05.41 Penzance–Paddington train, past Wootton Rivers on 3 October 2016 with power car No. 43144 bringing up the rear. Just to the right of the leading power car cab you may just be able to see the Kennet & Avon Canal. (Author)

First Great Western Class 153 No. 153370 passes the White Horse Business Park near Trowbridge, operating 2M11, the Swindon–Westbury, on 8 September 2014. (Author)

A bit of a Southern Region celebrity at the time was Class 33 No. 33008 *Eastleigh*, painted in this retro-green livery. On 10 April 1988, it is seen at Sherrington – between Warminster and Salisbury – while working the 14.44 Westbury to Portsmouth Harbour service. Just weeks later, these loco-hauled services between Portsmouth and Bristol/Cardiff would be replaced by new sprinter units. (Nic Joynson)

A very rare pair of visitors along the Waterloo to Exeter route in the form of Class 20s with No. 20904 *Janis* leading the Exeter to Westbury weed-killing train past West Hatch, near Tisbury, on 10 April 1991. To the rear is No. 20901 *Nancy*. At the time, the locomotives were owned by Hunslet-Barclay and named after female employees in its office. (Nic Joynson)

No. 37905 *Vulcan Enterprise* is photographed on Upton Scudamore bank on 4 July 1989 working 6O45, the 03.05 Cardiff Tidal Sidings–Hamworthy Goods. Unusually, on this occasion, this steel working conveyed Transit vans from the Ford plant at Bridgend for Southampton. (Steve McMullin)

A nice bit of vegetation clearance by Network Rail to the cess-side embankments at Wilton Junction allows long-lost photographic angles to once again be 'on'. However, it doesn't take long for Mother Nature to regrow so opportunities have to be taken quickly. On 4 May 2010, 7O48, the 09.22 Whatley Quarry–Hamworthy loaded stone train, hauled by No. 59104 *Village of Great Elm*, creeps round off the Down Westbury line at Wilton Junction, heading towards Salisbury in some great weather conditions. (Author)

Following accident damage, No. 47230 is seen receiving a new end cab at Swindon Works on 27 February 1985. However, this would be a short-lived repair as the Class 47 would be withdrawn from BR service during January 1987 and scrapped during March 1989. (Author)

The end of the line for Class 46 No. 46006 at Swindon Works on 27 February 1985. By the time this photograph had been taken, it had already been withdrawn for three years and, like the vast majority of the fifty-six-strong fleet of Class 46s, would be scrapped at Swindon Works – No. 46006's turn came five months after this photograph was taken, during July 1985. (Author)

Yet again, the overnight sleeper service from Penzance to Paddington failed to reach its destination – on this occasion due to a fault with the coaching stock. In order to balance out the stock for its next working, a short notice empty coaching stock move was arranged, running as 5A40 (10.55 Plymouth–Paddington) and hauled by Direct Rail Services No. 57310 *Pride of Cumbria*, as seen here on 24 November 2014, passing Great Cheverell. (Tom Curtis)

Due to engineering works between Castle Cary and Cogload Junction, Freightliner was obviously in desperate need of traction, leading to a rare outing for Network Rail's No. 57305, which is seen here climbing the bank at Upton Scudamore on 30 April 2013 with Freightliner-operated 6Z30, the 17.23 Westbury Yard–Eastleigh Yard. (Author)

Following an overnight covering of snow, the landscape around Barford St Martin is transformed as No. 50018 *Resolution* leads No. 50017 *Royal Oak* on 1O34, the 08.10 Exeter St Davids–Waterloo service, on 11 February 1991. No. 50018 *Resolution* was being worked up to Salisbury to replace No. 33109, which was on 1V11 (the 11.00 Waterloo–Exeter St Davids service), and to attach No. 50029 *Renown* which had failed at Salisbury the previous day. (Steve McMullin)

Old meets new at Swindon on 1 June 2017. New Hitachi-built Class 800 unit No. 800002 stands alongside the train it will soon replace, the 1970s-built High Speed Train with power car No. 43098 which is departing on a Paddington-bound service. (Steve King)

Owing to some recent tree clearance work, this long-lost shot from the Lady Down Aqueduct has become possible again. Seen here about to pass underneath the Kennet & Avon canal on 6 April 2015, No. 158950 heads away from Bradford Junction with the 14.30 Cardiff Central to Portsmouth Harbour service. (Dan Read)

Fairwood footpath crossing between Westbury station and Fairwood Junction is always a popular location to watch and photograph passing trains. Here a First Great Western HST passes over the crossing (on the right-hand side) on 3 December 2014, the winter light creating a nice glint on the power car. (Author)

GB Railfreight now has a toehold on Mendip aggregate workings. On 23 August 2016, No. 66750 *Bristol Panel Signal Box* is seen here running alongside the Kennet & Avon Canal as it approaches Crofton with 6V42, the 08.13 Wellingborough–Whatley Quarry stone empties. This particular locomotive previously saw work in mainland Europe and, as a result, has a number of detail differences such as rectangular buffers and Continental light clusters. (Dan Read)

One locomotive synonymous with Westbury during the 1980s was No. 47901. The Class 47 was a testbed for the proposed Class 58 and was re-engined with a Ruston-Paxman engine and renumbered from 47601 to 47901 in November 1979. Here, it is seen departing Westbury on 11 June 1987 with an unidentified stone working. The first Class 58 was introduced at the end of 1982, with deliveries of the fifty-strong fleet continuing until early 1987, and by March 1990 the unique No. 47901 had been withdrawn from service. (John Dedman)

Passing over Westbury North Junction on 11 June 1987 is No. 08935, hauling a short rake of MGR hoppers, presumably on a trip working from the cement works at Heywood Road Junction back to Westbury Up Yard. (John Dedman)

The Freightliner Class 70 locomotives are not a particularly common sight through the Wylye Valley. However, on 7 April 2015 Freightliner services were diverted via this route and No. 70007 is seen at Sherrington Lane hauling 4O54, the 06.12 Leeds Freightliner Terminal–Southampton Maritime Container Terminal train. (Tom Curtis)

First Great Western was rebranded Great Western Railway on 20 September 2015 and launched a new dark green livery. For the press launch, one HST set was turned out in the new livery and branding. Looking very spruce in its new GWR green livery on 23 September 2015, just three days after the launch, HST power car No. 43188 passes Highworth Junction in Swindon with power car No. 43187 trailing on 1L32, the 06.58 Swansea–Paddington service. (Steve King)

Under an incredibly dark and moody sky, a pristine No. 60051 *Mary Somerville* is pictured between Norton Bavant and Warminster on 18 April 1991 while working 6V13, the 12.24 Furzebrook–Hallen Marsh LPG train. This traffic ceased with the final train running on 22 July 2005, hauled by No. 66119. (Steve McMullin)

On 1 March 1991, No. 47564 *Colossus* sets back into Quidhampton Quarry with 6L07, the 12.36 Salisbury Yard–Quidhampton trip working. Upon return to Salisbury as 6L08 (the 13.13 Quidhampton–Salisbury), the wagons would then be marshalled into a Salisbury to Gloucester Speedlink trip. Quidhampton quarry, near Salisbury, saw its final train on 14 October 2009 when Western D1015 *Western Champion* took redundant china clay wagons down to Tavistock Junction. There are currently plans to fill in the site and then landscape over it with materials brought in by rail although, at the time of writing, this has yet to commence. (Steve McMullin)

Thursday 20 July 1995 was one of several days that week that high temperatures caused 7A09, the 07.05 Merehead–Acton Yard 'jumbo train', to be subjected to axle box checks at Westbury prior to onward movement. To the left, No. 59101 *Village of Whatley* is seen in the Down Reception with the 'jumbo'. Note the 'Not To Be Moved' board on the front of the loco while the shunter looks around the train. Meanwhile, Dutch-liveried No. 37371 arrives hauling failed No. 59103 *Village of Mells* on 7C29, the 05.40 Acton Yard–Whatley Quarry train, having dragged the formation down from Acton Yard. (Steve McMullin)

Severe weather conditions were certainly playing their part when this photograph was taken, and so much so that operators like Cross-Country were badly affected. Firstly, the seawall at Dawlish was breached by the sea, making national headline news at the time, and then flooding occurred in the Bridgwater area. As a result, all services started from Exeter St Davids and diverted via Westbury to Bristol. Here diverted Cross-Country 1S45, the 09.23 Exeter St Davids–Aberdeen train, which would normally have started from Plymouth, passes Fairwood footpath crossing while operated by No. 221138 on 25 February 2014. (Author)

The chimney of the Lafarge Cement Works at Westbury dominated the local landscape for some forty years. However, upon closure of the works in 2009 the chimney stood dormant until demolition on 18 September 2016. Some four months before demolition, EWS-liveried No. 66129 passes on 4 May 2016 while working 6A26, the 10.33 Whatley Quarry–Hayes & Harlington loaded stone train. Although cement is no longer produced at the site, it is still an active railhead. (Author)

Here, Nos 67023 and 67027 top and tail their four-coach test train past Yarnbrook – between Westbury and Trowbridge – on 22 March 2017, running as 1Z78 (the 06.05 Tyseley LMD–Bristol High Level Sidings via Westbury). The superbly cleared embankment is a result of extensive stabilisation work. The two Class 67s had recently been acquired by Colas from DB Cargo and this was their second day of operation with their new operator. (Tom Curtis)

History has a habit of repeating itself. A Class 56 thuds along Upton Scudamore bank with a train load of aggregate/ballast and only the brash livery of the current owners of the locomotive gives away the era. Colas Railfreight Class 56 No. 56087 – which has acquitted itself well since returning to service from scrap conditions – found itself in the Westbury area on 16 September 2013 and in charge of 6Z30, the 17.23 Westbury Yard–Eastleigh Yard engineers' train. (Tom Curtis)

No. 37175 heads away from Trowbridge – with its four-coach test train and classmate No. 37219 on the rear – on 5 October 2016 with 1Z78, the 06.43 Tyseley LMD–Bristol High Level Sidings. This is a regular test train that generally runs on a four-week cycle, heading to Weymouth and running out and back via Westbury. (Tom Curtis)

During November 2013, it was announced that Colas Railfreight would procure ten Class 70s; later this would increase to a fleet of seventeen locomotives, including one from Turkey that had been originally been built as a demonstrator. Although they can be found in many areas of the country on various types of workings, there is usually a high concentration of the class based at Westbury for use on engineering trains. On 25 May 2014, No. 70805 approaches Hawkeridge Junction at Westbury with an engineering train from Gaer Junction at Newport. (Tom Curtis)

The delightful Wylye Valley – between Salisbury and Warminster – is the setting for Royal Train locomotive No. 67006 *Royal Sovereign* on 24 January 2009 as it passes Hanging Langford while working 1Z80, the 09.39 Victoria–Bath Spa train, formed of the VSOE set. (Author)

A lovely fresh and crisp morning on the Berks & Hants route as the driver of Thames Turbo unit No. 166209 slows for Bedwyn on 8 March 2011. (Author)

The week commencing 16 March 1987 saw some additional/revised workings from Merehead quarry and during that first week there were a number of workings utilising pairs of Class 37s. On 17 March 1987, BR blue No. 37139 leads Railfreight grey No. 37695 towards Warminster with 6Z42 (the 13.34 Merehead–Eastleigh FY Sidings train), loaded with thirty-nine PGA type wagons and assisted by No. 56034 *Castell Ogwr Ogmore Castle* to the rear in full white-out conditions. The Class 56 on the rear banked the train as far as Warminster. (Steve McMullin)

Sporting the original Network South East livery is No. 50029 *Renown*, which is seen arriving at Salisbury on 12 October 1989 while working the 10.20 Exeter St Davids to Waterloo service. This particular Class 50 was to survive into preservation and can be found at Peak Rail in Derbyshire under ownership of the Renown Repulse Restoration Group, which is aiming to restore not only this locomotive but also classmate No. 50030 *Repulse*. (John Dedman)

Great Western Railway service 2V88 (08.53 Weymouth–Bristol Temple Meads), with hired-in Class 158 No. 158881 from South Western Railway, approaches Westbury at Fairwood footpath crossing on 6 November 2017. (Author)

Sporting a rather distinctive Maritime blue livery, which was applied at Eastleigh Works, is GB Railfreight Class 66/7 No. 66727 *Maritime One*, which is seen passing East Grimstead while working 6M46, the 12.13 Marchwood–Bicester train, on 22 February 2018. The locomotive was named on 20 September 2017 at the Birmingham Intermodal Freight Terminal. (Author)

The classic location of Crofton on the Berks & Hants route, between Bedwyn and Pewsey, on 21 April 2015 as 1C77 (the 10.06 Paddington–Penzance) sweeps round past a lock on the Kennet & Avon Canal. (Author)

Running some half an hour early past Crofton is 7C31, the 09.55 Theale–Merehead Quarry train, on 21 April 2015, worked by No. 59203. (Author)

Approaching Middle Road UWC (User Worked Crossing), at Bapton in the Wylye Valley, on 13 May 2016 is No. 159014, which is seen while working 1V33, the 13.52 Salisbury–Bristol Temple Meads service. (Author)

Direct Rail Services Class 47 No. 47853 *Rail Express* storms away from Swindon, near Blagrove, on 13 April 2014 with a Footex from Paddington to Swansea. (Steve King)

The view from Westbury station on 15 June 2013, towards the up yard, as No. 66115 approaches the signal with an engineers' train to Craven Arms. The somewhat squat looking shunter No. 08995 alongside looks a little odd compared to the Class 66. Three Class 08s were reduced in height during the 1980s for use on the Burry Port & Gwendraeth Valley Railway to Cwm Mawr in west Wales, to replace the ageing Class 03 shunters that were being phased out by British Rail. (Tom Curtis)

Due to closure of the line between Taunton and Bridgwater, Arriva Cross-Country services were diverted via Westbury, bringing the unusual sight of not only Cross-Country services via this route but one of their HST sets instead of the more regular Voyager units. On 18 February 2014, power car No. 43304 leads one such service from Exeter to Edinburgh past Fairwood footpath crossing on the approach to Westbury. (Tom Curtis)

Withdrawn Southern Region 4-EPB units Nos 5422 and 5404 are hauled by No. 47702 *County of Suffolk* past Bradford-on-Avon on 26 April 1994. A lot of Southern Region EMU stock was reaching the end of its working life and was worked under its own power to Eastleigh or Bournemouth for stripping before being hauled to Margam or MoD Caerwent for scrapping. This working was 7V15, the 09.28 Bournemouth T&RSMD–Margam TC (for Gwent Demolition). TC stands for 'Terminal Complex'. In years gone by that would have been something like 'Marshalling Yard' or 'Goods Yard' etc. (Steve McMullin)

Veteran Class 31 No. 31190/D5613 with a Railvac ready to depart from Westbury on 12 August 2013, bound for Washwood Heath in Birmingham. Beyond is another unusual sight these days for Wiltshire – Class 60 No. 60065 *Spirit of Jaguar*. (Tom Curtis)

A rare visit to the Wylye Valley on 2 November 2016 sees GBRf duo No. 73962 *Dick Mabbutt* and No. 73965 top and tail 1Q66, the 10.07 Woking–Westbury–Basingstoke–Eastleigh–Woking service, on a journey of some 219 miles. Here, No. 73962 *Dick Mabbutt* leads the return past Sherrington Lane near Codford on the return working from Westbury back towards Salisbury. (Author)

Another freight flow consigned to the history books – the Quidhampton tanks. With a suitably adorned home-made headboard reading 'Quidhampton 1972–2009', and black taped 'Last Quid' on the cab front, the final 6Y27 (10.12 Quidhampton–Eastleigh East Yard train) departs from Salisbury on 30 March 2009 with No. 66193 taking the honours. (Author)

No. 59103 *Village of Mells*, sporting the rather distinctive ARC mustard livery, passes Norton Bavant on 22 January 1992 while working 7O83, the 12.10 Whatley Quarry–Fareham loaded stone train. (Nic Joynson)

Traintours' 'The Desert Songster' railtour on 31 August 1987 brings the incredibly rare sight of a Class 40 to the Waterloo to Exeter route with No. 40122/D200 passing Barford St Martin between Salisbury and Tisbury. The tour had originated from Preston, running down to Kensington Olympia where Nos 73117 and 73119 would take the tour into London Waterloo. With the Class 40 on the opposite end at Waterloo, it then ran down to Exeter via Salisbury, then back via Taunton and Westbury to Reading before heading north back to Preston. No. 40122 was withdrawn during April 1988 and then entered into preservation. It is currently located at the National Railway Museum at York. (Nic Joynson)

BR blue No. 37273 and BR green No. 37350 power away from Bradford Junction on 16 May 1989 while working 6A18, the 04.35 Robeston–Theale Murco oil tanks. Three weeks later, trials commenced with nineteen 102-ton tanks to Theale in advance of Class 60s taking over the traffic. (Steve McMullin)

What has become a common sight, in one form or another, around the national railway network during autumn time is the Rail Head Treatment Train (or RHTT). This train blasts the railhead with highly pressured water to remove leaf mulch and other residues that stick to the rail, creating contamination and ultimately poor adhesion/ braking for trains. On 30 October 2017, one such train – 3J43 (02.53 Didcot Yard–Didcot Fuel Point via West Ealing and Swindon) – passes Crofton, hauled by No. 66119. To the rear is No. 66093. (Steve King)

During April 1986, the Bristol area civil engineers' saloon DW80975 was repainted into Inter-City livery. On 15 July 1986, the saloon is seen at Warminster with No. 47060 providing the traction for a 2Z01 Bristol to Bristol inspection via Merehead, Westbury, Warminster and Westbury. Approaching the inspection saloon from the Salisbury direction is No. 47232 with 6V79, the 09.07 Eastleigh Yard–Severn Tunnel Junction speedlink working. (Steve McMullin)

With the Iron Age Martinsell hill fort in the distance, a First Great Western HST passes New Mill, near Pewsey, on 2 March 2011. (Author)

A winter wonderland in the Wylye Valley on 9 January 2010 as a two-car Class 150 hurries past Little Langford. (Author)

Three-car Class 150 No. 150002 approaches Collins Lane Crossing, at Purton, on 19 November 2017 while working 2G85 the 14.34 Swindon–Cheltenham Spa service. (Steve King)

Preserved Western D1015 *Western Champion* is seen at Swindon Works on 27 February 1985 in a state of restoration. (Author)

The Didcot to Padworth and Westbury Merry-Go-Round (MGR) circuit ran as follows: outwards as 6A04, the 06.27 train ran from Didcot TC–Aldermaston–Padworth (Goodwins coal depot)–Westbury Up TC (for Westbury Cement Works) to Westbury North Junction. The return work was by 6A05, the 10.39 Westbury Up TC–Didcot TC train. On 10 December 1986, No. 58033 is captured approaching Westbury East Loop Junction, heading back with 6A05, which is formed of empty HTA-type MGR hopper wagons. (Steve McMullin)

Unusual traction for 7Z00 (the 09.47 Bridgwater–Winfrith flask train) on 14 June 1989 with engineers' DCWA sector Class 50 No. 50042 *Triumph*, which is seen passing Hawkeridge Junction. After a loco change at Westbury, it would be electro-diesel No. 73136 that would take the train forward to Dorset. (Steve McMullin)

Railfreight grey Class 56 No. 56041 passes over Fairwood Junction on 30 March 1990 with an unidentified stone working. (Tony Callaghan)

No. 37087 approaches Salisbury on 12 October 1989 with an additional Ministry of Defence trip, most likely from Dinton to Marchwood. (John Dedman)

A six-car Class 159 at Ford, near Salisbury, on 27 March 2008 is seen working the 06.20 Honiton to Waterloo service. (Nic Joynson)

Direct Rail Services Class 68s No. 68005 *Defiant* and No. 68001 make a change from the more usual Colas locomotives found on test trains as they pass Highworth Junction on 17 July 2016, the train running as 1Z16 (12.18 Reading Triangle Sidings–Derby RTC via Kemble). (Steve King)

A mere 441 minutes (or seven hours and thirty-five minutes) late, and passing Great Cheverell on 3 February 2012, is No. 66618 *Railways Illustrated Annual Photographic Awards – Alan Barnes* with 6V14, the 22.38 Stud Farm–Westbury Yard train, making this a rare daylight working. (Author)

Running some twenty-seven minutes early, DB Class 59 No. 59205 drifts past Drynham, on the outskirts of Trowbridge, on 8 September 2014 while working 6A83, the 13.26 Avonmouth–West Drayton service. (Author)

An additional service in connection with rugby in Cardiff on 9 February 2008 sees No. 67029 *Royal Diamond* pass the Kennet & Avon Canal at Crofton on a cold winter's morning, running as 1Z31 (Paddington–Cardiff Central), which is made up predominantly of ex-Virgin-liveried coaches. No. 67024 trails to rear. (Tom Curtis)

The Fridays-only 7O40 (13.35 Merehead Quarry–Eastleigh), worked by No. 59002 *Alan J. Day*, slowly climbs Upton Scudamore bank – between Dilton Marsh and Warminster – in a brief but welcome patch of sunshine on 19 May 2017. (Tom Curtis)

The former Great Western Railway works at Swindon undertook Class 08 overhauls right up until closure. Here, on 27 February 1985, one such example, No. 08702, looks to be about midway through its overhaul. Swindon Works would eventually close just over a year later on 26 March 1986. The site is now (as of March 2018) part retail outlet village, part steam museum, part housing and part commercial. (Author)

Four Class 40s await scrapping at Swindon Works on 27 February 1985; namely, No. 40149, followed by Nos 40176, 40154 and 40083. All were scrapped by the end of the year, except for No. 40149 which lasted until the May of the following year. (Author)

A rare working on the Berks & Hants route captured at the site of the former Grafton East Junction, from the now demolished occupation bridge, on 9 January 2014. West Coast Railways Class 33 No. 33029 *Glen Loy* is employed to move a crane running as 6Z47 (the 10.46 Westbury Yard–Woking Up Yard). (Steve King)

No. 33116 with its pair of 4TC sets gets away from Salisbury on 21 April 1989 with the 08.39 Yeovil Junction–Waterloo service. In the distance, another Class 33 and 4TC formation can just be seen going in the opposite direction towards Salisbury station. (Nic Joynson)

The new order on Great Western is the Hitachi-built Class 800 five-car units. Here, No. 800004 *Sir Daniel Gooch* passes Purton, on the approach to Swindon, running as 3X04 – the 14.10 Kemble–Paddington test run. Although not obvious, the name *Sir Daniel Gooch* is applied underneath the small cab-side window to the right of the driver's door, unlike a more traditional nameplate. (Steve King)

Class 45 D88 stands at Westbury during August 1969 on an unidentified parcels working. Under the TOPS renumbering of the early 1970s this would become No. 45136, remaining in British Rail service until withdrawal on 7 May 1987. Final disposal would come during March 1992. (Tony Callaghan)

D1054 *Western Governor* stands in the Up Yard at Westbury during the spring of 1975 with a stone train from the Mendip quarries. Within a year, this locomotive was to end up in the scrap line at Swindon Works to meet its final fate and was no more by May 1977. Of interest are the staff uniforms of the day – not an item of orange hi-vis clothing, or hard hat, to be seen – compared to the modern railway of today. (Tom Curtis)

The impressive and almost cathedral-like signal box at Westbury, which came into use from 14 May 1984, dominates the shot on 30 June 2015 as No. 59202 *Alan Meddows Taylor-MD, Mendip Rail Limited* passes while working 6C76, the 14.40 Acton Yard–Merehead Quarry train. (Steve Clark)

Scratchbury Hill dominates the backdrop at Norton Bavant, near Warminster, as No. 66206 is seen leading Tuesdays-only 6V62 (the 09.18 Fawley–Tavistock Junction tanks) on 18 January 2011. This service ceased with the final train out of Fawley on 29 October 2013. (Author)

Off their usual route via Didcot and Swindon, due to engineering works, and instead diverted via the Berks & Hants route through Pewsey and on via Bradford-on-Avon are the Saturday 6B33, the 11.27 Theale–Margam tanks, which are seen here on 24 January 2015 worked by No. 60054 on the approach to Woodborough loop. (Author)

Not a common sight at Westbury station: the sight of two Aggregate Industries Class 59s side by side. On 3 June 2017, No. 59005 *Kenneth J. Painter* (left) shunts wagons while No. 59002 *Alan J. Day* (right) is stabled between duties alongside. (Steve King)

A westbound First Great Western HST passes Callow Hill, to the west of Royal Wootton Bassett, on the 'top road' from Swindon to Bristol Parkway on 24 August 2010. (Author)

A rare sight of a pair of Class 20s passing through Wiltshire. On 25 February 2014 London Transport-liveried No. 20189 leads BR blue No. 20142 past Fairwood footpath crossing on the approach to Westbury, hauling No. 47375 *Tinsley Traction Depot*, No. 31459 *Cerberus* and No. 47769 *Resolve* and running as 0Z20, the 07.45 Okehampton–Derby Gas Tank Sidings train. Incredibly, in October 2015 the centre locomotive, No. 47375, was exported to Hungary for use with Continental Rail Solutions. (Author)

Nos 47286 and 47379 on the Highworth branch on 16 November 1998 with the 08.15 Swindon–Longbridge car train from the nearby Honda plant in Swindon. (Nic Joynson)

Original Railfreight grey-liveried Class 31 No. 31185, with the Bristol area civil engineers' inspection saloon, DW80975, runs off the East Chord at Bradford North Junction on 23 April 1987 while running as 2Z01, the 08.45 Bristol Temple Meads–Salisbury–Westbury–Bristol Temple Meads train. (Steve McMullin)

No. 56049 arrives at Westbury on 1 November 1984 with an unidentified working. To the right is the small stabling point at Westbury with two Class 37s and a 47 visible on shed. This small depot closed on 1 March 1993. The site these days is devoid of all buildings but is predominantly occupied by Colas Railfreight which generally has several Class 70s stabled there. (John Dedman)

Finished in retro BR blue and grey, power car No. 43002 *Sir Kenneth Grange* passes Highworth Junction, on the approach to Swindon, on 24 May 2016 while leading 1B45, the 10.45 Paddington–Swansea service. (Steve King)

Following engineering work near Wanstrow, on the Merehead branch, No. 59103 *Village of Mells* heads back to Westbury with the first train out of the possession. It is seen here at Fairwood footpath crossing on 26 February 2012. (Tom Curtis)

No. 59201 *Vale of York* leads No. 59001 *Yeoman Endeavour* on 11 October 2010 towards Crofton with 7A17, the 10.31 Merehead Quarry–Acton Yard service. Note the commemorative bell above the cab windscreens and below the horn grill. It was a tradition by General Motors to fit a bell to a new customer's locomotive. No. 59201 was originally owned and operated by National Power before EWS took over its operations and fleet of six Class 59/2s. (Author)

It doesn't get much rarer than this: on 11 June 1985 Class 45 No. 45143 was diagrammed to work from Exeter to Waterloo and back to Exeter in connection with a renaming ceremony at Waterloo to celebrate the 300th anniversary of the Battle of Waterloo. Working up on the 05.48 Exeter St Davids to Waterloo service, No. 45143 would be named *5th Royal Inniskilling Dragoon Guards 1685–1985* by the Duchess of Westminster at Waterloo. Specially turned out by Toton depot, the immaculate No. 45143 stands at Salisbury on the return working; 1V13, 13.10 Waterloo–Exeter St Davids. (Author)

Passing East Grimstead on 19 May 1993 is No. 37705, which is working 6V62, the 10.34 Fawley–Tavistock Junction train formed of locomotive fuel oil and bitumen. To the right is the connection into East Grimstead quarry, which has since been closed. However, the ground frame by the concrete hut is still in use to operate an emergency crossover, situated where the Class 37 is positioned. (Steve McMullin)

Privately owned by the Scottish Thirty-Seven Group, but on long-term hire to Colas Railfreight, is No. 37025 *Inverness TMD*, which is seen here arriving at Westbury on 26 May 2016 while working 3Z14, the 09.54 Bristol Barton Hill–Weymouth–Bristol High Level Sidings train. (Steve Clark)

A cold and crispy morning for this very rare working on 20 January 2011 as No. 56312 (ex-No. 56003) hauls Colas track machines DR92377, DR92400, DR76601 and tail gunner No. 47739 *Robin of Templecombe* past Fairwood footpath crossing, running as 6Z76, the 07.35 Tavistock Junction–West Ealing train. (Author)

With so few Class 60s in service by 2011, it was unusual to find one operating out of the Mendip quarries. On 8 March 2011, No. 60013 *Robert Boyle* finds itself working 6A74, the 09.22 Whatley Quarry–Theale train, and is seen here rounding the curve towards Crofton up the classic Berks & Hants route. (Author)

A unique livery at the time was that carried by DB Schenker Class 60 No. 60040 *The Territorial Army Centenary*, which is seen here on 3 May 2011 approaching Westbury. (Tom Curtis)

The year 1987 was the penultimate year of newspaper trains on British Rail. With a uniform rake of all-blue NJV and NKV vans, with some branded 'newspapers', No. 50041 *Bulwark* and No. 50033 *Glorious* double-head 3A27, the 06.50 Plymouth–Paddington empty newspaper vans, along the Westbury-avoiding line on 10 February 1987. All such traffic ceased to run the following year. (Steve McMullin)

A lucky patch of sun after some rain showers, greets retro-green-liveried No. 47812/D1916 at Norton Bavant on 25 September 2012 as it passes with 5Z47, the 13.35 Bristol Temple Meads–Eastleigh depot train, formed of the stock that normally works the 'Torbay Express'. However, the operating season had drawn to a close and the stock was being returned to Eastleigh for winter storage. (Author)

Compared to the image above, it's incredible how much vegetation has grown over the years alongside the railway line, completely changing the appearance of the same location. Here, No. 56034 *Castell Ogwr Ogmore Castle* passes Norton Bavant on 18 April 1989 with 7O83, the 12.09 Whatley Quarry–Fareham stone working, passing the same spot as the Class 47 in the previous image. (Nic Joynson)

The Network Rail NMT, or New Measurement Train, makes a regular visit once every four weeks to the Westbury area. On 5 May 2016, it is seen on Upton Scudamore bank heading away from Dilton Marsh and towards Warminster, led by power car No. 43062 *John Armitt*. To the rear is power car No. 43014 *The Railway Observer*. There are three power cars in use for this train with one usually undergoing maintenance while the other two are in service. (Dan Read)

All is perhaps not quite as it seems with No. 37705 at Warminster on 9 April 1990. Having been worked up the previous evening from Tavistock Junction, it should have been the job of the Class 08 shunter at Westbury to trip this trainload of tracked military vehicles into Beechgrove Sidings at Warminster. However, the train was over-length and beyond the capabilities of the shunting locomotive so No. 37705 was removed from the Ripple Lane to Frome bitumen tanks to trip the train up from Westbury to Warminster, making this a rare working for a petroleum sector Class 37. (Steve McMullin)

Beautiful Wiltshire countryside surrounds Tisbury and passing Tisbury West crossing, about a mile west of Tisbury station, is No. 47702 *Saint Cuthbert* with the 08.10 Exeter St Davids to Waterloo service on 15 August 1991. (Nic Joynson)

No. 50001 *Dreadnought* passes Hatch, to the west of Tisbury, on 1 November 1988 while working the 09.10 Waterloo to Exeter St Davids. (Nic Joynson)

On a sweltering 6 August 1992, No. 73131 *County of Surrey* in Dutch livery passes Sherrington, in the Wylye Valley, with a Winfrith to Gloucester working conveying two nuclear flasks. (Nic Joynson)

At their final resting place, awaiting scrapping at Swindon Works, on 30 October 1985 are Nos 25326 and 25258. No. 25258 would be gone four months later during February 1986, with No. 25326 hanging on a bit longer, with final disposal coming during November 1986. (John Dedman)

On 29 January 1986, Class 56 No. 56034 *Castell Ogwr Ogmore Castle* passes Little Cheverell with a Westbury Up Yard to Woodborough wagon test train formed of five PIA-type Tiphook wagons and an ex-Southern Railway brake van in Railfreight Construction livery. The Tiphook wagons later entered service at both Merehead and Whatley Quarries. The wagons were later converted to HQA/JJA-type discharge wagons for Railtrack which in turn has since become Network Rail. (Steve McMullin)

Pictured in nice lighting conditions are this pair of veteran Brush Type 4s, with No. 47739 *Robin of Templecombe* top and tailing No. 47749 *Demelza* on two barrier coaches – Nos 6330 and 6348 – from Bristol to Eastleigh Works on 16 December 2011. The move was in readiness of transferring some redundant First Great Western HST buffet cars to Kilmarnock where they would then be converted into standard coaches with a full seating type arrangement. (Tom Curtis)

With storm clouds and rain having recently passed, No. 159020 passes Sherrington while working 1O48, the 12.51 Bristol Temple Meads–Salisbury train, on 20 December 2013, bringing behind it some fine sunny weather. (Author)

While hauling the return leg of the Belmond British Pullman excursion from Bath on 21 June 2017, No. 67003 developed a problem and was subsequently declared a failure. Classmate No. 67015 was run round from the rear to the front of the train at Westbury – up until then the train being in top and tail operation with the Class 67s – to then take the train forward. Working hard to raise its train up the gradient, No. 67015 is seen leading No. 67003 through Old Dilton with 1O92, the 15.55 Bath Spa–London Victoria train, which at this point is running some sixty-five minutes late. (Dan Read)

Displaying its unique London Transport Museum livery, GB Railfreight-operated Class 66 locomotive No. 66718 *Sir Peter Hendy CBE* is seen here on 13 March 2017 heading along the 1900-opened Stert and Westbury route as it passes Cowleaze Lane in Edington with 6V42, the 08.13 Wellingborough–Whatley train, consisting of empty aggregate box wagons. (Dan Read)

A tense moment between the clouds on 6 November 2017 at Fairwood Junction as 7C31 – the 09.55 Theale–Whatley Quarry train – passes by, hauled by No. 59203. (Author)

On 6 August 1998, EWS-liveried No. 37411 *Ty Hafan*, which is hauling the six-coach 11.02 Weymouth to Bristol Temple Meads service, comes over Fairwood Junction heading for Westbury station. (Nic Joynson)

As part of the Easter 2013 blockade of Reading station, due to station redevelopment works, many First Great Western services were altered and operated over diversionary routes. A near-hourly service between Devon and Cornwall to London Waterloo was operated over one such diversionary route. Taking the booked route as far as Westbury, services would then reverse before running to Waterloo via Salisbury, Andover, Woking and Clapham Junction. On Good Friday 29 March 2013, power car No. 43168 leads 1V36, the 10.07 Waterloo–Plymouth service, through the Wylye Valley at Bapton, between Salisbury and Warminster. (Author)

A bit of human interest as a couple of volunteers from the Kennett & Avon Canal Trust prepare to open the lock gates at Freewarren Lock on 21 April 2015 for a narrowboat heading along the canal as No. 66143 passes by hauling 6M20, the 08.14 Whatley Quarry–St Pancras loaded stone train. (Author)

With a trainload of empty Dogfish hopper wagons, No. 50046 *Ajax* stands at Westbury on 5 April 1990, presumably after a change of drivers. The train had departed Westbury two hours earlier with a fully loaded train, only to return empty, so presumably a ballast drop had taken place in the local area. (John Dedman)

The rundown of the Cardiff Cathays Works prior to closure in mid-1993 saw the contract for the overhaul of RES/Royal Mail vehicles transfer to Eastleigh Works with movements between Bristol Barton Hill and Eastleigh via Westbury. On 6 September 1996, RES-liveried No. 47536 passes Heywood village, north of Westbury, while working 5V96, the 16.08 Eastleigh Works–Bristol Barton Hill train formed of three pristine TPO vehicles. (Steve McMullin)

No. 47063 sweeps around towards Crofton on 3 May 1990 with an eastbound stone train out of the Mendip quarries. (Nic Joynson)

Dutch-liveried No. 33019 *Griffon* takes an Eastleigh to Meldon Quarry engineers' train away from Westbury South Junction and down towards Fairwood Junction on 20 February 1992. (Nic Joynson)

From the small fleet of five Class 59/0 locomotives, No. 59002 *Alan J. Day* approaches Fairwood Junction on 6 November 2017 while working 7B12, the 11.35 Merehead–Wootton Bassett loaded stone train. This is the site of the water troughs that ran from Fairwood Junction towards Fairwood Crossing (now known as Masters Crossing) during the days of steam; one of the water tower bases can just be seen to the left of the Class 59 which had recently been revealed after vegetation clearance by Network Rail's contractors. (Author)

Is it in Hampshire or is it in Wiltshire? Practically straddling the county boundary is No. 60045 *The Permanent Way Institution*, passing Dean – between Romsey and Salisbury – with a short load of just two flat wagons loaded with track panels on the daily engineers' train (6V41, 14.45 Eastleigh Yard–Westbury Yard) on 4 September 2013. (Author)

Running just under two hours early is No. 56312 *Jeremiah Dixon–Son of County Durham–Surveyor of the Mason-Dixon Line USA*, looking and sounding fantastic with 6Z56, the 12.50 Long Marston–Totton Yard train, on 20 September 2013. The gleaming Class 56 sports the new DCR grey livery and is seen passing Sherrington, between Warminster and Salisbury. The wagons were being moved to the Southampton area in connection with a new DCR (Devon & Cornwall Railway) contract on the Network Rail Wessex Route for use with the Railvac machine. (Author)

No. 56056 passes some lovely rosebay willowherb on the site of the former Wolfhall Junction on 31 July 1986. (Tony Callaghan)

The first EW&S-liveried Class 37, No. 37057 *Viking*, leads No. 37137 past Highworth Junction while hauling a failed No. 60094 *Tryfan* and forty-five loaded HBA covered hopper wagons with 6A64, the 07.40 Avonmouth–Didcot Power Station train, on 10 July 1996. The two Class 37s had been dispatched from Didcot to assist the Class 60, which had failed in Hullavington loop. (Steve McMullin)

Running about three hours late on 19 March 2009, and hauled by No. 66707 *Sir Sam Fey – Great Central Railway*, GB Railfreight stock positioning move 5V60 (10.20 Eastleigh Depot–Bishops Lydeard) passes Little Langford. (Author)

Members of staff from the Canal & River Trust look on as No. 66092 sweeps round past Crofton with 6V33, the 11.05 Wembley Yard–Whatley Quarry service, on 27 March 2017. (Author)

With No. 43152 trailing, uniquely liveried power car No. 43172 *Harry Patch – The Last Survivor of the Trenches* leads 1A81, the 08.44 Penzance–Paddington service, towards Fairwood Junction on 23 November 2017 in some superb light which shows off the black livery of the power car well. (Author)

Making its way along the Melksham single line, Colas Railfreight-operated No. 70802 is seen here passing Monkton, Broughton Gifford, on 17 April 2016 as it hauls 6C22, the 09.00 Alstone (Cheltenham) to Westbury (via Stroud and Swindon) train of Coalfish wagons loaded with ballast spoil. (Dan Read)

Looking very smart in its BR blue livery is No. 47270 *Swift*, which is seen departing Swindon's Cocklebury Sidings on 12 July 2010 with a 5Z29 empty coaching stock move to Crewe, despite the headcode panel displaying 1Z60. (Steve King)

It's 10 September 1992 and No. 59004 *Yeoman Challenger* approaches Warminster with a Merehead to Eastleigh loaded stone train. (Nic Joynson)

A trip working off the Gloucester to Eastleigh Speedlink working was 6A60, the 08.55 Westbury Up TC–Melksham, conveying bagged fertiliser traffic. Having arrived on 8 March 1989, worked by No. 37429 *Eisteddfod Genedlaethol,* the return working departs Melksham as 6A61 (10.00 Melksham–Westbury Up TC) conveying three empty wagons. The fertiliser silos on the right have since been demolished and the site closed. (Steve McMullin)

Single line working is in operation over the Down Trowbridge line between Bathampton Junction and Bradford West Junction due to plain line track renewals of the Up Trowbridge line at the site of the former Limpley Stoke station. Passing the worksite is No. 47567 *Red Star* running wrong-road with the Sunday 2O87 (the 09.10 Bristol Temple Meads–Weymouth train) on 3 September 1989. (Steve McMullin)

Unlike the green livery of Freightliner, which tends to blend into the surroundings, the new red livery of DBS stands out well in the surrounding countryside. At the time (13 October 2009), the sole DBS-liveried Class 66 No. 66152 is seen here on the Tuesday-only 6V62 (08.48 Fawley–Tavistock Junction train) at Hanging Langford. (Author)

Pressed into active service almost immediately after it arrived off transfer from the Midlands two days previously, No. 150122 powers (probably for the first time ever) up Upton Scudamore bank on 19 October 2011 while working the 14.59 Frome to Warminster service; from Warminster it will return as the 15.28 to Great Malvern. A lucky break in the cloud allows this dramatic and colourful shot against the moody dark sky beyond. (Tom Curtis)

No. 47083 *Orion* is seen working 3A27, the 06.15 Plymouth–Paddington parcels train, as it hammers over Fairwood Junction on 6 June 1984. The signal box had been decommissioned a couple of weeks earlier, on 14 May 1984, as part of the Westbury area re-signalling scheme. Demolition was soon to follow. (John Dedman)

'Hampshire' unit DEMU No. 205027 runs into Salisbury's platform 6 on 28 April 1987. Headcode '87' indicates this a Portsmouth to Salisbury or Westbury via Netley slow service. (Author)

Who could have imagined it? Thirteen years after withdrawal, Warship D818 *Glory* was to be scrapped at Swindon Works. Mass withdrawal of the thirty-eight-strong fleet had seen them all taken out of service by 1972 with D818 *Glory* being stopped on 1 November 1972. Here, work is progressing on 30 October 1985 with its scrapping and not much is left to identify what it is. (John Dedman)

Hopes of preserving this locomotive – which had been 'adopted' by staff at the works and had even had a repaint even though it was withdrawn – did not come to fruition. Keeping unusual company with a Class 27 on the Swindon Works scrap line, D818 *Glory* is seen on 30 October 1985, thirteen years after it was withdrawn from service. (John Dedman)

On 23 May 1989, Class 47 No. 97561 was named *Midland Counties 150 1839–1989* at Derby, to celebrate the 150th anniversary of the Midland Counties Railway between Nottingham and Derby, and sported a maroon livery. A week later, on 30 May 1989, and still looking immaculate, the locomotive passes Bradford Junction in charge of 1Z16, the 07.50 Derby–Bath Spa charter via Westbury, to run round. Although designated a Class 47, it was classified as '97' to reflect its status as a departmental locomotive associated with Derby RTC. (Steve McMullin)

Pathfinder Tours' 'The Hampshire Hotchpotch' 1Z61, the 06.23 Crewe–Southampton Western Docks, passes Norton Bavant, near Warminster, on 5 May 2012, hauled by Nos 20312 and 20308. Trailing out of sight to the rear is No. 37409. (Tom Curtis)

ADB 977695, aka 'the Swedish Scrubber', was converted from parcels van No. 94001 at A. B. Mahler & Son, Rossor, Sweden. Upon return to the UK, it was repainted into Network South East livery. During the 1991 leaf fall season, which commenced from October 1991, it operated with the Derby RTC Tribology test train, plus two vehicles from 4TC set No. 8012. Traction was provided by specially converted, and dedicated, Class 33/1 No. 33102, which is seen on 29 November 1991 passing Wilton South while working 'Circuit 46', running from Eastleigh via Laverstock, Andover, Basingstoke, Salisbury, Tisbury and back to Eastleigh. The 'Swedish Scrubber' is immediately behind the locomotive. (Steve McMullin)

During 1992, the Exeter Area Civil Engineer took over responsibility for track renewals from Sherborne to Wilton Junction. On 12 November 1992, the first inspection special ran to Salisbury with No. 37092 and inspection saloon DB999509 operating as 2Z01, the 08.34 Exeter St Davids to Salisbury and return train, which is pictured here on the return to Exeter, passing the former Wilton South station. (Steve McMullin)

Diverted off its more normal route is Freightliner's 4O57, the 13.29 Wentloog–Southampton Maritime train, which is seen passing the site of Oaksey station on 22 September 2016, hauled by No. 66529. Oaksey Halt, located on the Swindon to Kemble route, closed on 2 November 1964. (Steve King)

Hertfordshire Railtours' 'Baker's Dozen' railtour on 28 June 1987 with No. 45128 is seen at Westbury station. The railtour did not get off to a good start when original train locomotive No. 45062 failed 10 miles out of Euston station, requiring assistance from a pair of Class 31s as far as Birmingham New Street where No. 45128 would then continue on back to London Waterloo. With the Class 45s in the twilight of their operational lives, and following its failure on this tour, No. 45062 would be taken out of traffic almost immediately. No. 45128, however, would soldier on a little longer until withdrawal during April 1989. (Author)

Hanson-liveried No. 59104 *Village of Great Elm* is seen here heading past Langley Burrell, near Chippenham, on 18 February 2016 with 6Z48, the 09.30 Appleford–Whatley Quarry train of empty aggregate box wagons. The earlier than usual pathway from Appleford provided a welcome morning westbound working of interest along this route. The shot is taken from the bridleway bridge that replaced the automatic half barrier level crossing here when the line speed was upgraded prior to the introduction of HST services in the 1970s. (Dan Read)

Having only been in service for some six months, No. 159002 is seen passing Hanging Langford on Christmas Eve 1993, working a Southampton to Cardiff service. (Nic Joynson)

One of the recently acquired Class 60s by Colas Railfreight from DB Cargo is No. 60076, which is captured here passing the site of the former Wolfhall Junction near Savernake on 9 May 2015 while working 6V62, the 11.18 Tilbury–Llanwern steel train. (Steve King)

Having just departed from Westbury Yard, and over the avoiding line flyover, recently repainted No. 66041 eases the daily engineers' working 6O41, the 10.14 Westbury Yard–Eastleigh Yard train, up towards Dilton Marsh, past Penleigh, on 18 April 2017. (Author)

With some quite obvious front-end damage (caused during a shunting accident at Lackenby steelworks during October 1981), No. 40193 awaits its turn for scrapping at Swindon Works on 27 February 1985. Final disposal would follow during July 1986. (Author)

1A78, the 06.45 Penzance–Paddington train, comes over Fairwood Junction, near Westbury, on 30 October 2017, led by GWR green power car No. 43188, complete with its Y Cymro/The Welshman dragon insignia. Out of sight, to the rear, is power car No. 43127 *Sir Peter Parker 1924–2002 Cotswold Line 150* which is carrying the more standard First Great Western blue livery, in keeping with the rest of the set. (Author)

It was always going to be 'all or nothing' here on 30 April 2013 with the prospect of three freights in quick succession and from both directions. First up is No. 66080, which is seen passing Upton Scudamore while hauling a nice uniform rake of yellow JNAs loaded with ballast – presumably for the Castle Cary to Cogload Junction possession – and running as 6Z58 (14.45 Eastleigh Yard–Westbury Yard). (Author)

A faded Southern Region 'Thumper' DEMU approaches Taw Valley Halt, on the Swindon & Cricklade Railway, on 22 March 2015. (Steve King)

HST power car No. 43021 passes a very wintry Highworth Junction on 7 January 2010 with a westbound service from Paddington. (Steve King)

As part of the GWR 150 celebrations during 1985, a small event was held at Salisbury by British Rail, the GWR having had a presence in the city with its own terminus station until closure in October 1973. The GWR station site was to eventually develop into what is now the Class 159 depot site, opening in 1993 for the new units on the Waterloo to Exeter route. On display, and presenting a rather unusual sight in the east end bay of Salisbury on 14 August 1985, are No. 47158 *Henry Ford*, No. 37244, No. 33008 *Eastleigh* and a 'Thumper' unit, No. 1128. To the left is shunter No. 09001. (Author)

With acres of rapeseed throughout the Wylye Valley, it certainly makes for a very colourful scene at this time of year. Passing one such field is No. 59001 *Yeoman Endeavour* on 21 April 2015 as it heads past Bapton working 7V07, the 12.41 Chichester–Merehead returning stone empties. (Author)

On 19 June 1990, Class 50 No. 50019 *Ramillies*, one of the Civil Engineers' DCWA fleet of Class 50s, rounds the curve into Melksham station with 7Z50, the 09.30 Bristol East Depot–Westbury–Melksham–Swindon–Westbury–Bristol ballast drop, which is formed of five ZFV Dogfish and four YGB Seacow wagons. With one wagonload of ballast already having been discharged between Bradford Junction and Melksham, the remaining would be required for discharge between Swindon and Thingley Junction on the return. (Steve McMullin)

Running seventy minutes late, the daily Freightliner trip passes Fairwood Junction, at Westbury, on 25 February 2014 with No. 66617 in charge of 6C72, the 08.20 Fairwater Yard–Westbury Yard HOBC. (Author)

No. 66556 certainly isn't hanging about on 8 September 2014 as it passes Thingley while working 4L32, the 11.00 Bristol FLT–Tilbury loaded Freightliner service. (Author)

The view from Masters Crossing, just west of Fairwood Junction, on 23 November 2017 as GBRf-operated 6V42 (the 08.13 Wellingborough Up Yard–Whatley Quarry train) passes by, worked by No. 66732 *GBRf The First Decade 1999–2009 John Smith MD*. Breaking the DB-Cargo mould on the Mendip quarry traffic, this GB Railfreight-operated train runs approximately one week in four. (Author)

The Wiltshire Somerset & Weymouth Railway opened its line from Thingley Junction to Westbury, with intermediate stations at Melksham and Trowbridge, on 5 September 1848. To commemorate the 150th anniversary of its opening, a commemorative run took place on 5 September 1998 formed of No. 153353 carrying dignitaries and members of the public. Here, the single-car unit passes the site of Broughton Gifford Halt, which closed on 7 February 1955, running as 2Z70, the 11.17 Westbury–Chippenham–Westbury service. Note the special headboard marking the event in the cab window. (Steve McMullin)

Well, this was an unexpected bonus! Expecting the more usual EWS-liveried Class 66, it was in fact DB Schenker red Class 59/2 No. 59206 *John F. Yeoman – Rail Pioneer* that came into view past Little Langford on 3 February 2012 with a mixed bag of wagons while working 6O41, the 10.14 Westbury Yard–Eastleigh Yard engineer's train, in stunning winter light. (Author)

On 9 August 1990, Her Majesty the Queen travelled to Devizes for an official reopening ceremony at Caen Hill locks, on the Kennet & Avon Canal, following extensive renovation and restoration. Travelling by the Royal Train, No. 47835 *Windsor Castle* is seen passing Crofton heading for Pewsey, where the royal party would then continue by road to Devizes. (Steve McMullin)

Westbury 'super shunter' No. 60007 *The Spirit of Tom Kendell* propels its train of wagons back into the yard at Westbury station on 26 May 2016. (Steve Clark)

This working was a fairly short-lived flow: 7O92, the 17.53 Taunton Fairwater Yard–Horsham Up TC train via Warminster with products from the now closed Taunton Civil Engineers Concrete Works. On 19 June 1990, No. 33025 *Sultan* is seen on Upton Scudamore bank at Old Dilton with a trainload of STV tube wagons. (Steve McMullin)

Stunning weather on 14 April 2015 as one of Colas Railfreight's small fleet of just five Class 66s, No. 66850 *David Maidment OBE,* passes Old Dilton. This Colas-operated working forms the second of two daily engineers' services to run along the Wylye Valley, the train running as 6O31 (17.34 Westbury Yard–Eastleigh East Yard). Note the Balfour Beatty crane and support vehicles forming part of the consist. (Author)

Sporting the long obsolete Great Western Trains franchise ivory and green livery, HST power car No. 43040 passes Wolfhall on 16 November 1998 while leading the 08.05 Penzance–Paddington service. The franchise began operating from February 1996 but by December 1998 had become First Great Western following First Group's buyout of its partner's shares in Great Western Holdings. With it came a change in name for the franchise and a change of livery, the ivory and green soon passing into history. (Nic Joynson)

A new era for Great Western, and train travel through Wiltshire, is the introduction of the new Hitachi-built Class 800 Inter-City Express trains or IET. At the spiritual home of the GWR, Swindon, a pair of these new units, led by No. 800006 with No. 800013 behind, awaits departure on 30 November 2017 while working 1B28, the 11.45 Paddington–Swansea service. (Mark Pike)

On 20 January 2017, and in bitterly cold but stunning winter light, Colas Railfreight Class 70 No. 70802 sweeps round past Avoncliff with nineteen PGA-type four-wheel cement wagons running in what has become a regular Friday working; 6C36, the 12.20 Westbury LaFarge Sidings–Aberthaw LaFarge Sidings train. (Author)